Baby's name:..

Useful information:

Baby's date of birth..

Birth weight...

Baby's National Health Service number..................................

....

Doctor's phone number..

Feeding method...

Record of baby's weight:

Date								
Weight								

Date								
Weight								

Date								
Weight								

Newborn Twins Daily Journal.

Congratulations on the arrival of your little babies. Your world is about to change in the most extraordinary, wonderful and sometimes most overwhelming way. Jotting down information about your babies day can help you work out what your little ones need and remember what they have done…so when the midwife asks how many wet nappies your babies have had today, or you try to remember which breast which baby last fed from, the information is at your fingertips in your Daily Journal. This journal will help you to discover and track changes in your babies natural routines should you so wish. It may also help you to pinpoint your babies' needs so that you can respond calmly and lovingly and will hopefully give you encouragement and reassurance when you look back in your journal you can see how much progress your babies have made.

This journal records the basic daily tasks such as feeding (for breastfed babies record which side baby fed from and for how long, bottle fed babies quantity of milk consumed), nappies (wet and soiled), how much awake time each baby has, when the babies sleep and for how long. Finally the 'other' column can be used for a variety of information – baby's temperature, any medication given, general hygiene (bath / top and tail) and any unusual behavior. The journal can be used by anyone caring for the babies and can be a useful tool for handovers between parents and other people caring for the twins. The pages are set out so that you can record the information for each baby on opposing pages so that you can at a glance look at both babies' notes hopefully making it easier to keep track.

I hope that you will find it useful!

Xx Caroline

Baby's name:...

Useful information:

Baby's date of birth..

Birth weight..

Baby's National Health Service number.............................

....

Doctor's phone number...

Feeding method...

Record of baby's weight:

Date								
Weight								

Date								
Weight								

Date								
Weight								

Baby’s name:

Date	Time	Feed Details	Awake	Sleep	Nappies	Other

Additional information:

Baby's name:

Date	Time	Feed Details	Awake	Sleep	Nappies	Other

Additional information:

Baby’s name:

Date	Time	Feed Details	Awake	Sleep	Nappies	Other

Additional information:

Baby's name:

Date	Time	Feed Details	Awake	Sleep	Nappies	Other

Additional information:

Baby's name:

Date	Time	Feed Details	Awake	Sleep	Nappies	Other

Additional information:

Baby's name:

Date	Time	Feed Details	Awake	Sleep	Nappies	Other

Additional information:

Baby's name:

Date	Time	Feed Details	Awake	Sleep	Nappies	Other

Additional information:

Baby's name:

Date	Time	Feed Details	Awake	Sleep	Nappies	Other

Additional information:

Baby's name:

Date	Time	Feed Details	Awake	Sleep	Nappies	Other

Additional information:

Baby's name:

Date	Time	Feed Details	Awake	Sleep	Nappies	Other

Additional information:

Baby's name:

Date	Time	Feed Details	Awake	Sleep	Nappies	Other

Additional information:

Baby's name:

Date	Time	Feed Details	Awake	Sleep	Nappies	Other

Additional information:

Baby's name:

Date	Time	Feed Details	Awake	Sleep	Nappies	Other

Additional information:

Baby's name:

Date	Time	Feed Details	Awake	Sleep	Nappies	Other

Additional information:

Baby's name:

Date	Time	Feed Details	Awake	Sleep	Nappies	Other

Additional information:

Baby's name:

Date	Time	Feed Details	Awake	Sleep	Nappies	Other

Additional information:

Baby’s name:

Date	Time	Feed Details	Awake	Sleep	Nappies	Other

Additional information:

Baby's name:

Date	Time	Feed Details	Awake	Sleep	Nappies	Other

Additional information:

Baby’s name:

Date	Time	Feed Details	Awake	Sleep	Nappies	Other

Additional information:

Baby's name:

Date	Time	Feed Details	Awake	Sleep	Nappies	Other

Additional information:

Baby's name:

Date	Time	Feed Details	Awake	Sleep	Nappies	Other

Additional information:

Baby’s name:

Date	Time	Feed Details	Awake	Sleep	Nappies	Other

Additional information:

Baby’s name:

Date	Time	Feed Details	Awake	Sleep	Nappies	Other

Additional information:

Baby's name:

Date	Time	Feed Details	Awake	Sleep	Nappies	Other

Additional information:

Baby's name:

Date	Time	Feed Details	Awake	Sleep	Nappies	Other

Additional information:

Baby's name:

Date	Time	Feed Details	Awake	Sleep	Nappies	Other

Additional information:

Baby's name:

Date	Time	Feed Details	Awake	Sleep	Nappies	Other

Additional information:

Baby's name:

Date	Time	Feed Details	Awake	Sleep	Nappies	Other

Additional information:

Baby’s name:

Date	Time	Feed Details	Awake	Sleep	Nappies	Other

Additional information:

Baby's name:

Date	Time	Feed Details	Awake	Sleep	Nappies	Other

Additional information:

Baby's name:

Date	Time	Feed Details	Awake	Sleep	Nappies	Other

Additional information:

Baby's name:

Date	Time	Feed Details	Awake	Sleep	Nappies	Other

Additional information:

Baby's name:

Date	Time	Feed Details	Awake	Sleep	Nappies	Other

Additional information:

Baby's name:

Date	Time	Feed Details	Awake	Sleep	Nappies	Other

Additional information:

Baby's name:

Date	Time	Feed Details	Awake	Sleep	Nappies	Other

Additional information:

Baby's name:

Date	Time	Feed Details	Awake	Sleep	Nappies	Other

Additional information:

Baby's name:

Date	Time	Feed Details	Awake	Sleep	Nappies	Other

Additional information:

Baby's name:

Date	Time	Feed Details	Awake	Sleep	Nappies	Other

Additional information:

Baby's name:

Date	Time	Feed Details	Awake	Sleep	Nappies	Other

Additional information:

Baby's name:

Date	Time	Feed Details	Awake	Sleep	Nappies	Other

Additional information:

Baby’s name:

Date	Time	Feed Details	Awake	Sleep	Nappies	Other

Additional information:

Baby's name:

Date	Time	Feed Details	Awake	Sleep	Nappies	Other

Additional information:

Baby’s name:

Date	Time	Feed Details	Awake	Sleep	Nappies	Other

Additional information:

Baby's name:

Date	Time	Feed Details	Awake	Sleep	Nappies	Other

Additional information:

Baby's name:

Date	Time	Feed Details	Awake	Sleep	Nappies	Other

Additional information:

Baby's name:

Date	Time	Feed Details	Awake	Sleep	Nappies	Other

Additional information:

Baby's name:

Date	Time	Feed Details	Awake	Sleep	Nappies	Other

Additional information:

Baby's name:

Date	Time	Feed Details	Awake	Sleep	Nappies	Other

Additional information:

Baby's name:

Date	Time	Feed Details	Awake	Sleep	Nappies	Other

Additional information:

Baby's name:

Date	Time	Feed Details	Awake	Sleep	Nappies	Other

Additional information:

Baby's name:

Date	Time	Feed Details	Awake	Sleep	Nappies	Other

Additional information:

Baby’s name:

Date	Time	Feed Details	Awake	Sleep	Nappies	Other

Additional information:

Baby’s name:

Date	Time	Feed Details	Awake	Sleep	Nappies	Other

Additional information:

Baby's name:

Date	Time	Feed Details	Awake	Sleep	Nappies	Other

Additional information:

Baby’s name:

Date	Time	Feed Details	Awake	Sleep	Nappies	Other

Additional information:

Baby's name:

Date	Time	Feed Details	Awake	Sleep	Nappies	Other

Additional information:

Baby’s name:

Date	Time	Feed Details	Awake	Sleep	Nappies	Other

Additional information:

Baby's name:

Date	Time	Feed Details	Awake	Sleep	Nappies	Other

Additional information:

Baby's name:

Date	Time	Feed Details	Awake	Sleep	Nappies	Other

Additional information:

Baby's name:

Date	Time	Feed Details	Awake	Sleep	Nappies	Other

Additional information:

Baby’s name:

Date	Time	Feed Details	Awake	Sleep	Nappies	Other

Additional information:

Baby's name:

Date	Time	Feed Details	Awake	Sleep	Nappies	Other

Additional information:

Baby's name:

Date	Time	Feed Details	Awake	Sleep	Nappies	Other

Additional information:

Baby's name:

Date	Time	Feed Details	Awake	Sleep	Nappies	Other

Additional information:

Baby's name:

Date	Time	Feed Details	Awake	Sleep	Nappies	Other

Additional information:

Baby's name:

Date	Time	Feed Details	Awake	Sleep	Nappies	Other

Additional information:

Baby's name:

Date	Time	Feed Details	Awake	Sleep	Nappies	Other

Additional information:

Baby's name:

Date	Time	Feed Details	Awake	Sleep	Nappies	Other

Additional information:

Baby’s name:

Date	Time	Feed Details	Awake	Sleep	Nappies	Other

Additional information:

Baby's name:

Date	Time	Feed Details	Awake	Sleep	Nappies	Other

Additional information:

Baby’s name:

Date	Time	Feed Details	Awake	Sleep	Nappies	Other

Additional information:

Baby's name:

Date	Time	Feed Details	Awake	Sleep	Nappies	Other

Additional information:

Baby's name:

Date	Time	Feed Details	Awake	Sleep	Nappies	Other

Additional information:

Baby's name:

Date	Time	Feed Details	Awake	Sleep	Nappies	Other

Additional information:

Baby’s name:

Date	Time	Feed Details	Awake	Sleep	Nappies	Other

Additional information:

Baby's name:

Date	Time	Feed Details	Awake	Sleep	Nappies	Other

Additional information:

Baby’s name:

Date	Time	Feed Details	Awake	Sleep	Nappies	Other

Additional information:

Baby's name:

Date	Time	Feed Details	Awake	Sleep	Nappies	Other

Additional information:

Baby's name:

Date	Time	Feed Details	Awake	Sleep	Nappies	Other

Additional information:

Baby's name:

Date	Time	Feed Details	Awake	Sleep	Nappies	Other

Additional information:

Baby’s name:

Date	Time	Feed Details	Awake	Sleep	Nappies	Other

Additional information:

Baby’s name:

Date	Time	Feed Details	Awake	Sleep	Nappies	Other

Additional information:

Baby’s name:

Date	Time	Feed Details	Awake	Sleep	Nappies	Other

Additional information:

Baby's name:

Date	Time	Feed Details	Awake	Sleep	Nappies	Other

Additional information:

Baby's name:

Date	Time	Feed Details	Awake	Sleep	Nappies	Other

Additional information:

Baby's name:

Date	Time	Feed Details	Awake	Sleep	Nappies	Other

Additional information:

Baby's name:

Date	Time	Feed Details	Awake	Sleep	Nappies	Other

Additional information:

Baby’s name:

Date	Time	Feed Details	Awake	Sleep	Nappies	Other

Additional information:

Baby’s name:

Date	Time	Feed Details	Awake	Sleep	Nappies	Other

Additional information:

Baby's name:

Date	Time	Feed Details	Awake	Sleep	Nappies	Other

Additional information:

Baby’s name:

Date	Time	Feed Details	Awake	Sleep	Nappies	Other

Additional information:

Baby's name:

Date	Time	Feed Details	Awake	Sleep	Nappies	Other

Additional information:

Baby’s name:

Date	Time	Feed Details	Awake	Sleep	Nappies	Other

Additional information:

Baby's name:

Date	Time	Feed Details	Awake	Sleep	Nappies	Other

Additional information:

Notes.

www.ingramcontent.com/pod-product-compliance
Ingram Content Group UK Ltd.
Pitfield, Milton Keynes, MK11 3LW, UK
UKHW021051270726
13967UKWH00012B/454

9 781326 456917